God is Love

God is Love

Short stories of Gods redeeming work in the lives of women and what they tell us about the character of God

Compiled by Tolu Oyelowo

With Contributions from:

Tammy Anderson

Rosaline Brown

Comfort Cobblah

Patty Doyle

Kirstin Jackson

Judith (Judi) Johnson

Damaris Mkubwa

Kemi Okoya

Fereshteh Shahabi

Patricia Welsh Brown

And others who wish to remain Anonymous

Copyright © 2015 by Tolu Oyelowo

All rights reserved

This book or any portion thereof may not be reproduced or used in any manner whatsoever without the express written permission of the author or publisher

Scripture quotations used in this book are from The Holy Bible: New King James, New International and Message Versions, as retrieved from BibleGateway. (www.biblegateway.com)

Books may be purchased at Amazon.com.
For quantity and/or special sales purchases; contact the publisher: www.createspace.com/pub/l/createspacedirect.do?rewrite=true
Fax: (206) 922-5928, Attn: CreateSpace Direct Reseller program

ISBN-13: 978-1512300871

Printed in the United States of America

Dedication

I dedicate this book with gratitude to the giants on whose shoulders I stand. My mother, Mrs. Olanike Oyelowo, who taught me that if I look around and see no one, I can always look up; my sister Joy Oyelowo, who taught me that there is joy in suffering, joy in pain, joy in patience, and joy in perseverance. My family, whose faith remains a source of daily encouragement to me, and the "sista's" who shared their stories with me, To God be the Glory!

The Character of God
From Psalm 145

I will exalt you, my God the King;
I will praise your name for ever and ever.
Every day I will praise you
and extol your name for ever and ever.
Great is the LORD and most **worthy** of praise;
his **greatness** no one can fathom.
One generation commends your works to another;
they tell of your mighty acts.
They speak of the **glorious** splendor of your majesty—
and I will meditate on your wonderful works
they tell of the **power** of your **awesome** works—
and I will proclaim your great deeds.
They celebrate your **abundant goodness**
and joyfully sing of your **righteousness**.
The LORD is **gracious** and **compassionate;**
slow to anger and **rich in love**.
The LORD is **good** to all;
he has **compassion** on all he has made.
All your works praise you, LORD;
your faithful people extol you.
They tell of the **glory** of your kingdom
and speak of your **might**,
so that all people may know of your mighty acts
and the glorious splendor of your kingdom.

Your kingdom is an everlasting kingdom,

and your dominion endures through all generations.

The LORD is **trustworthy** in all he promises

and **faithful** in all he does

The LORD **upholds** all who fall

and **lifts up** all who are bowed down.

The eyes of all look to you,

and you **give them their food** at the proper time.

You open your hand

and **satisfy the desires** of every living thing.

The LORD is **righteous** in all his ways

and **faithful** in all he does.

The LORD is **near** to all who call on him,

to all who call on him in truth.

He **fulfills the desires** of those who fear him;

he **hears their cry and saves them.**

The LORD **watches** over all who love him,

but all the wicked he will destroy.

My mouth will speak in praise of the LORD.

Let every creature praise his **holy** name

for ever and ever.

CONTENTS

Introduction 1

God is Righteous 3
Thirty five and Single 4

God is Protector 6
Driving Home in a Winter Blizzard 7
In an Instant 9

God is Love 11
Mother-Daughter Shopping Day 12

God is Merciful 15
The Prodigal 16

God is Compassionate 19
Ministry 20

God is Trustworthy 22
Mr. Smith 23

God is Sovereign 27
Why I need Jesus 28

God is Abundantly Good 31
The Price of Education 32

God is Peace 37
The Stroke 38

God is Worthy 42
Adoption 43
God's Abounding love 44
Love in Action 45

God is Glorious 47
Daddy Taught Me 48

God is Father 50
Parenting 51
Saying Goodbye to Dad 53

God is Healer 57
This Illness is not to Death 58

God is Provider 60
The Home Search 61

God is Restorer 64
Restored Back to Life 65

God is Creator 68
Encounters 69

God is Near 72
Needing Wisdom 73

God is Omnipotent (Almighty) 77
Emma 78

God is Everlasting 82
Life is a Marathon 83

God is Awesome 88
Miracle Child 89

God is Faithful 93
A Cure for Busy-ness 94

God is Grace 99
A New Life 100

Bibliography 106

Introduction
God Is Love

I remember the first time I heard the story of Rahab. I had a long commute to and from work, and had decided that I would use the time to read/listen to the bible on tape. Having completed the Old Testament, I was starting on the New Testament. The book of Matthew begins with the genealogy of Jesus Christ.

It is a long list of names, and I wasn't fully paying attention, but then I heard a name that caused me to pull over on the side of the road and listen again. "Salmon had Boaz (**his mother was Rahab**), Boaz had Obed (Ruth was the mother), Obed had Jesse, Jesse had David, and David became king.

That day, I learned something about love in action. The bible tells us that **"God so loved the world that he gave his only son, that whosoever believes in him will not perish but have everlasting life."**

In the story of Rahab, we learn that all the other inhabitants of Jericho were destroyed by Joshua and his army. However Rahab and her family were saved; because she placed her faith; hung her hope in God.

The book of Joshua: Chapter 6

"Only Rahab the prostitute and all who are with her in her house shall be spared, because she hid the spies we sent.

So the young men who had done the spying went in and brought out Rahab, her father and mother, her brothers and sisters and all who belonged to her. They brought out her entire family and put them in a place outside the camp of Israel.

But Joshua spared Rahab the prostitute, with her family and all who belonged to her; because she hid the men Joshua had sent as spies to Jericho"

In this story, a woman's love for her family, spurred her on to an act of courage based on faith. That act would save her and her entire family from destruction; and change the trajectory of her life. So it was that a woman shunned by society would become the great-great grandmother of the greatest King of Israel, and ancestor to Jesus the Christ; son of God; savior of the world.

It is my prayer that as you read these stories, and see God at work in the day to day lives of women, your faith in God will increase, and that increase will motivate you to act. Act by receiving God's gift of love in Christ Jesus and act by attending to Gods whisper in your ear, to go and demonstrate love to the world.

God is Righteous

Thirty Five and Single

It's been challenging, and it's starting to feel lonely. I am tired of having dinner by myself; tired of sitting alone on Easter and mother's day and thanksgiving, tired of always being the one to have to reach out to people. Just tired.

I recall a book I was given by my pastor when I was single and twenty nine, a book written by a flight attendant who talked about being single and in her mid-thirties. I remember particularly when she stated that she had learned to talk to God about her most intimate thoughts and what a difference that made. I had tried it then, and decided to try it again. "God, I am lonely. God I am tired. God I desire intimacy. God I want to be held. God I am lonely. "

Off to sleep. I still believe he would send angel Gabriel to knock me out because I slept so deeply, I frequently overslept. I would wake up the next morning late for work with no time to feel bad about being alone.

As it turned out there were two men in my life soon thereafter, and I now had to make a decision as to who I wanted to date. Here is the surprise; that was even lonelier. That is when I realized that these men simply didn't 'get me' the way Jesus did. I had to explain myself to them. Jesus on the other hand knew me so well; he would explain me to me. It was time to harness that special bond and work on having my most intimate relationship with Jesus.

Prayer: from the song - Have Faith in God

"Have faith in God when your pathway is lonely he sees and hears all the way you have trod. Never alone are the least of his children. Have faith in God, have faith in God. Have faith in God, he's on his throne, have faith in God he watches o'er his own, he cannot fail, he must prevail. Have faith in God, have faith in God."

Strengthen my faith Lord and sanctify me. Amen

God is Protector

Driving Home in a Winter Blizzard

The commute from home to work was an hour and a half each way. It was Friday and time to head back home. It was snowing which was nothing new, but the roads were surprisingly slippery. I knew this because at my very first stop light I found I couldn't stop the car. It kept sliding into the intersection. Amazingly I was not struck; instead all the other cars maneuvered themselves around me. I mentally geared myself up for a long slow ride home.

What I didn't anticipate was how bad that snow storm would become. I was on the freeway, and just like that I couldn't see a thing; it was a complete white-out. The snow was coming down so heavily, I may as well have been driving with my eyes closed. I could turn back and try to make it back to the office, but I couldn't see the exit, or I could keep going and hope I was keeping a straight line on the freeway – it didn't matter I couldn't see in front of me either. I started to panic. What if there was a big truck coming behind me; I was driving so slowly they would run right into me. What if I wasn't driving in a straight line? On either side of the freeway was a drop off; what if I drove right off the freeway into that drop off. I started to scream out prayers. "Lord help me!" "Lord I can't see – help me". I screamed so loudly, my voice became hoarse. And then I saw it. Off to the right side a small light. Ok – I could at least use that as the guide. I drove towards the light, but then I had to keep driving and the light wasn't there anymore, so I started screaming again –"Lord help me"; and there it was, that small light again. I drove towards it and then remembered what it was; highway markers, little posts on the side of the highway that I had seen in the past and never paid attention to.

I would use those markers as my guide for the next few hours. Each time I would see one, I would drive towards it, but then I would see nothing and start screaming prayers again, and just in time there would be another one. Each time it required driving towards the light, passing the light and experiencing a sense of blindness for just a few minutes, and then seeing the light again. I would continue this faith journey until I got home.

Those lights guided me over the ninety miles of freeway that led to my home. When I pulled up in my driveway, it was going on 11 p.m. The hour and a half drive had taken over four and a half hours.

As I listened to the radio that night, I learned that the freeway I was on had been closed. Driving conditions were so bad that the Department of Transportation had shut it down for that evening. I didn't know that; but I learned a valuable faith lesson. Sometimes God provides just enough light for us to take the next step. We may not have the light to see the entire journey, but if we take the first step towards the light that we do see, the next step becomes more visible. One step at a time till the journey is done' never forgetting that his banner of protection is over us.

Prayer from: Psalm 27:1-2
The Lord is my light and my salvation, I shall not fear. The Lord is the strength of my life, I shall not be afraid. Amen.

In an Instant

The day started like any other day. I was on my way to work doing battle with my toddler who had other plans for his day. Plans that had nothing to do with going to his day care. So as usual we were rushing. He is dressed. He is in the car, strapped into his car seat – Victory!

I had brought some food into the car as he had not yet eaten that morning. I turn around to feed him and he wants to eat. So we take a few minutes to have breakfast. He is done eating, looks happy and I decide to run back into the house to drop off the dirty dish and then take off.

I do just that, but when I come out thirty seconds later, the car is no longer in the garage. I run out of the garage, and can't believe my eyes. The car is hanging off the ravine outside our home! The side my son is strapped in is the side that is off the ravine. In that instant my world stopped. It was just an instant.

Angels must have been assigned to him that day because there was nothing stopping the rest of the car from falling off the ravine. Absolutely nothing! But it was stopped.

There are construction workers down the road. I yell to them to please help. I ask them to sit in the driver's seat while I pull my son out from his car seat just to ensure there is some weight on the opposite side. They say no way (and in hind sight I understand why) but they offer to stand outside and hold the door and the steering wheel.

I reach in and pull my screaming child out of his car seat.

I call a tow truck. Remarkably the car remains in place. The tow truck arrives, and he is able to pull the car off the ravine and on to the pavement. Everyone breathes a sigh of relief.

    I still tremble when I think of how that seemingly "normal" day could have turned out. But mostly I am grateful – so very grateful for the God who saw fit to protect my child that day. To his name be the glory! Give thanks to the Lord for he is good.

Prayer from: Psalm 136

Give thanks to the Lord for he is good, his mercy endures forever. Give thanks to the God of Gods, his mercy endures forever. Give thanks to the Lord of Lords, his mercy endures forever. To him who alone does great wonders; his mercy endures forever. Amen.

God is Love

Mother-Daughter Shopping Day

I was living away from home at college and missed my family. I prayed that God would allow me the opportunity to do 'girl' things with my mom. I especially wanted/craved a mother-daughter shopping day, although since my mother was living on another continent thousands of miles away I couldn't see how that would happen.

Fast forward about 20 years. Mom and I were now living together. It was an awful day weather-wise. It was Christmas Eve and we were in the middle of a heavy snow fall when mom announced –"I would like to go shopping." What! The weather is terrible. "I would like to go shopping" she repeated. Ok I said shopping it is.

The entire time we were out, I had a bad attitude. I tried to hide it, but I just couldn't believe she had picked one of the worst weather days of the year to decide she wanted to go shopping. She didn't say anything, but spent the day hand-picking her Christmas gifts that year.

We are done shopping and are driving home when in the quiet stillness of the car, my memory reaches back, and I am reminded of my prayer from decades prior. This was the mother/daughter girls shopping day that the lonely teenager had requested of God. I couldn't believe it. The prayer had been answered in an unexpected way, and here I was, missing my blessing because of a bad attitude. I realized then, that even the minutest of prayers are heard by God, and he always answers, sometimes in ways we don't expect.

As it turns out, that was my mother's last Christmas on earth. She would die several months later. I will always be grateful that I had that snowy winter shopping day with her. The day I almost missed out on because of a bad attitude. I cherish her Christmas present to me from that year – the gift she had selected, by herself, on 'girls' shopping day. More than that, I cherish the lesson she taught me; which is that love is the lens through which life must be lived. By her examples, her sacrifices, her courage, her strength, I learned the power of love. On that particular day, she put up with her daughters bad attitude because she wanted to fulfill an act of love. Truth be told though, that was just one small example of how she lived her entire life.

I am also grateful that our God is a God who answers prayers. Whenever I use the gift, I remind myself that God moves in mysterious ways, but his lens is always "love". Love conquered death; love pushed back evil, love is triumphant, love is victorious, love is peace, love is wealth and love remembers.

The cries of that lonely teenager like all of our prayers are heard, and answered. That said; on a practical level, love comes in many ways. I need to have an open heart so I don't miss the blessing. God moves in mysterious ways, his wonders to perform.

Prayer: from Psalm 116

I love the Lord for he heard my voice; he heard my cry for mercy.

Amen.

God is Merciful

The Prodigal

I had made some mistakes along the way and had done some things that I was not proud of. I was convinced I could not be forgiven; would not be forgiven because after all I knew better. That was until the day I wondered into a church in the inner city.

The pastor had a habit of taking an altar call at the end of the service. This church, I would later learn rarely/never closed a service without giving people a chance to repent and rededicate their lives to God. That day I felt the tugging on my heart. This was my day to take the walk down to the altar and rededicate my life to God. But it was a big church, and the thought of the long walk down to the altar was more than I could handle. I decided I would stay firmly in my seat. But then I heard the pastor say something like, "I feel the spirit is speaking to someone in this place today. So we will just wait for you to come on down."

I decided that person was me and stepped out into the aisle. (I remember stepping out into the aisle, and I remember standing at the front of that alter; I don't remember the walk down.) I was assigned to a counselor who prayed with me and listened to my confession. She was just the counselor I needed because everything that I had done wrong, she claimed she had done also – only worse. She looked at me and said "Christ forgave me, and if he forgave me, I am sure he will forgive you." Right there and then I asked for and received Christ's forgiveness.

For me, the amazing thing was learning that Gods love does not stop at forgiveness. Following mercy, there is redemption and following redemption there is restoration; undeserved, unearned, but boldly given in love.

Prayer from: Psalm 51

Have mercy upon me Oh Lord according to your loving kindness

According to the multitude of your tender mercies

Blot out my transgressions,

Wash me thoroughly from my sin

Create in me a clean heart oh God. Amen

God is Compassionate

Ministry

On a Sunday morning, I was standing close to the entryway of the church when a church member walked in. I had learned recently that her husband had taken ill, and so inquired about her husband. She informed me that he had died. I was stunned and must have worn that expression on my face because she wound up giving me encouraging words as she walked to her seat.

About half an hour later, I looked over at her and realized she was sobbing. I could tell this from her body movements. I started to pray that God would comfort her. A few minutes later, I looked up to see another church member get up from the other end of the sanctuary and come marching over. She sat next to this woman and gathered her up in her arms and just held her and allowed her to cry.

I was both grateful and embarrassed. Lessons learned - there is a time for everything; a time to pray and a time to act. What that woman needed that morning was exactly what she got; from the woman who came over from across the room to physically offer her comfort. She needed arms wrapped around her like her husband may have done – to comfort, encourage and love on her.

Sometimes we are called to pray; sometimes we are called to be Gods hands and feet. My task that day was not solely to pray. My task was to pray and then get up, get off my seat, and go and do something! Demonstrate love in a physical, tangible way.

Prayer: From 1 Corinthians: 13

Lord fill me with your love today, and then help me to demonstrate it in a tangible way to others. Thank you. Amen.

God is Trustworthy

Mr. Smith

I was a young college student who had come from Iran to study in the United States. Shortly after I left my country in 1978, the revolution of Iran began, the Shah left the country, the Ayatollah came into power and the hostage crisis made headlines in the news around the world. At the time I had no family or close relative in the United States. As a newcomer to the country, I had not yet been able to establish my support system and I was fully dependent on my parents financially.

After the revolution, there were many restrictions with regards to transferring funds abroad and as a result there were major delays for money transfers to students' accounts. At that time, even though my father had sent me money, the wire was not received by my bank for a couple of months. So there I was a twenty year old female student who could hardly speak English with no family or close relatives to turn to and with no money.

To deal with this madness, I used to walk to the bank everyday hoping that if the staff at the bank saw me in person they would check my account more closely and they would give me the good news (this was way before internet and ATMs). The amount of money I was expecting was $4000.00.

Making constant trips to the bank resulted in my meeting an older gentleman who was working there and became somewhat familiar with my situation. He reassured me that he would check my account every day and when the wire hit my account he would call me. His name was Mr. Smith. I suppose he must have felt sorry for me; after all, who in their right mind would take a walk to the bank in the brutal winters of Duluth, Minnesota.

His offer was very sweet but it didn't stop me from making the trip to the bank regularly as I desperately needed money to pay for my rent and tuition. One day when I walked into the bank Mr. Smith pulled up a chair and asked me to sit down. With great enthusiasm I asked him if he had good news for me. As he shook his head, he said no. When he witnessed the disappointed look on my face he asked me in a very caring and gentle voice if he could trust me. I was not sure what he meant by that but my answer was "yes, you can trust me." After confirming with me the dollar amount of the expected wire, he asked me to wait right there. He returned to his desk about twenty minutes later with some papers in his hands. He then sat down and told me "I am signing up for a loan for you, the $4000.00 will be in your account in a few minutes. Just promise me that when your money gets here you'll pay me back." He was not co-signing the loan; he was getting a loan for me as I did not have either a social security number or established credit.

For a second I saw my own father with all his love and support in this strange man. Being speechless I thought to myself, "is he my guardian angel or am I dreaming?" Well he was a man of his word. Within a few minutes, there it was $4000.00 in my account. That money in 1979 was enough to buy a brand new car. I thanked him in disbelief and left the bank.

By that Friday, the wire I was expecting arrived and Mr. Smith called me. I rushed to the bank, gave him his money back and to show my gratitude I invited him and his wife to dinner at the best restaurant in town. He smiled and gracefully declined my invitation. He then explained to me the concept of paying it forward. He went on to say that when he was a young man he was in need of some money and a total stranger helped him out without any expectation. Since then he promised himself if he was ever in a position to help others he would do it. Then with a smile he encouraged me to go home and think about whether I would want to make the same promise to myself. I thanked him again and I left the bank. I didn't need to think about it I wanted to be just like him; I wanted to be able to help others.

    Now thirty some years later I am thinking what a valuable lesson Mr. Smith gave me. Catherine Ponder says: "No one is your enemy, no one is your friend; everyone is your teacher." A couple of years later he retired and left the bank but his memory and his generous gesture made an amazing impression on me. I truly believe that at the time Mr. Smith was chosen by God to solve my problem. I also believe it is an honor and privilege to be chosen by God to be an instrument to touch people's hearts and impact their lives miraculously.

Prayer: From Proverbs 11:25

Help me God to bless others so that I may be abundantly blessed and help me to help others and in so doing be helped. Amen.

God is Sovereign

Why I need Jesus

I gave my life to Christ as a teenager but every once in a while I am struck by how much I need Jesus. I woke up one morning feeling like I needed the Lords blessings in a special way. So I opened my bible and read a few passages that described the Lords promises of blessings to his children. It may have been the day but every one of the blessings I read was conditional. If you obey…then, if you obey, then…, if you obey my commandments, then….

I decided I had better read the commandments over again to make sure I was in obedience to them. This is what they said:

You shall have no other gods before me.

You shall not make for yourself an image in the form of anything in heaven above or on the earth beneath or in the waters below.

You shall not misuse the name of the Lord your God

Remember the Sabbath day by keeping it holy. Six days you shall labor and do all your work, but the seventh day is a Sabbath to the Lord your God. On it you shall not do any work

Honor your father and your mother

You shall not murder

You shall not commit adultery

You shall not steal

You shall not give false testimony against your neighbor

You shall not covet your neighbor's house…..or anything that belongs to your neighbor.

I found it sobering as I realized that at some point in my life, I had failed on every single count. And that is when I 'got it' yet again. I had been a Christian for over three decades at the time, and I still failed on every single commandment. I get it. I need Jesus. I need someone to atone for my sins, because I cannot in my own flesh live up to any of Gods standards. 'No not one' is the way the bible describes humanity. Not one of us is worthy. Thank God for Jesus.

Prayer: from the song "I Need Thee"

I need thee every hour. Stay though nearby, temptations lose their power when though art nigh. I need thee, oh I need thee. Every hour I need thee. Oh bless me now my Savior. I come to thee. Amen.

God is Abundantly Good

The Price of Education

Ezra 8:22 ….the hand of God is upon us for good... (Message version: Our God lovingly looks after all those who seek him)

I started the process of applications for my child's school, eventually narrowing it down to five schools of choice. The application process to qualify for admission is an arduous task in itself and with very limited spaces to be filled by the institutions. Applicants and their parents are required to write essays; references must be obtained from various teachers in the current school as well as written tests and interviews.

It was an intense period with so much going on; it became a challenge to get everything done. At a point I began thinking of the application fees for each school, which was an expense we could do without at the time. The application cost brought everything into perspective☺. I said to my daughter, we are only applying to one school and we will trust God that if it's the school of his choice they will give you admission. She was terrified at the risk of having just one school option! I said to her, we pray and put it in God's hands. If they don't accept you, it's not the school for you and it's not God's will.

As of the date of deadline for submission, we didn't have all the items ticked off to put in the application. It was a Friday and in my panic, I decided that I would at least make the application fee payment with the hope that if they received it, we would appear prepared. We would then take a gamble on the lateness of submission of all other requirements.

On trying to make the payment online, there was an IP address error and it would not go through so I called the school to tell them I was having challenges with their system of payment and as such I was unable to go to the next step which is to submit. They were completely apologetic and said I should call the school on Monday to make payment and they would certainly accept the application at the same time and not reject it as being late. God in action! He gave us two more days of grace to finish our submission.

A month later my daughter received an admission letter. She cried and cried with joy and relief. She thought she hadn't done well in her one on one interview and was amazed at all the great things her interviewer had to say in her admission letter.

I am amazed and humbled by God's love for me. If we only trust him enough he will do as his word says.

Ephesians 3: 20 "…..him who is able to do immeasurably more than all we ask or imagine…." (Message version: God can do anything, you know------ far more than you could ever imagine or guess or request in your wildest dreams!)

On getting the admission, my husband and I assessed our finances and concluded we could not financially afford for our daughter to join the school and we would need to decline the admission. As you can imagine we were heartbroken to say the least!

A few days before deadline to accept or decline the application, I was having a conversation with God about it, asking him why it had all worked out this way when I clearly felt he had orchestrated things thus far. His answer for me was that we should apply to the school for financial aid. Financial aid applications had closed two months earlier so I was thinking 'how can I apply for aid when applications have closed?' The voice was clear and insistent. I told my husband what I was being ordered to do by the Holy Spirit but told him instead I would just ask them if my daughter's application could be deferred for a year.

I was so reluctant to do this that I waited until the day before the deadline to call the admissions director. My pitch to them was a request for deferment of admission and at the end of that I very timidly slotted in that I was wandering if we would be able to apply for financial aid. What baffled me was her response. It was as though she never heard my request for deferment. She jumped straight unto the financial aid question and told me to apply immediately. She said it was late but she would do all that she could to see what could be done.

For the next three days and nights and I mean that literally, I worked on filling the forms which were so tedious. I would start working on them online from 8 a.m. till evening; exchange information with my husband at night, then edit till 2 a.m. the next morning. In between, the school contacted me to say we should hurry with the submission as they wanted to be sure to have some funds reserved for our child.

Even as I write this testimony, I still have tears in my eyes because within twenty four hours of submitting the application; to the glory of God, our application was approved and my daughter was granted the scholarship she needed to attend the school. Our application was late and quite frankly we didn't even have some of the supporting documents we were supposed to provide. This could only have happened because God's unprecedented favor was in action. Trust in the Lord. Even in your darkest hour, trust in the Lord.

Prayer: From Proverbs 3:5 – 6 and the song Banner over me is love

Lord, please help me today to trust you with all my heart.

Help me to stop trying to figure things out on my own.

Help me to run to you, and run away from evil.

Help me to listen for your voice in everything I do knowing that you will keep me on track.

Help me also to accept your discipline knowing that even when you discipline, your banner over me is love. Amen.

God is Peace

The Stroke

A defining moment in my life was when I was in despair over what I had lost after having a stroke in my early fifties. I needed to grieve my losses yet was afraid that if I did I would find myself wallowing in grief with no way out. I am a Christian; I knew that God had not abandoned me. I felt His presence in my life and prayed often. Yet I could not take the time and energy, or the confidence to face my losses. Perhaps I was afraid? Perhaps I would not be able to rebound after facing these losses. I had lost all of me!

It was nearly eighteen months after my stroke. I had been working hard in rehabilitation the entire time to regain what I had lost. Progress had slowed way down and I needed to face my loss of "who I had been". Yet I could not do it because then I was giving up hope of recovery. Throughout these months I had been positive, very active and involved in my recovery. I was not mad or angry with God for what had happened to me. In fact, I felt reassured that God was with me and heard my prayers. Yet, my doctor said that I was depressed and she would like me to see a counselor. But why, I was not depressed. Yet I went---and cried through several sessions with the therapist. I was broken, never to be the same again.

I sat in church on the evening of Ash Wednesday. I heard my pastor talk about the symbolism of the ashes. After receiving communion we were invited to run our fingers through a bowl of ashes as we returned to our seats. I could not do it---those ashes were literally me! The verse "from dust we come and from dust we shall return" ran through my mind. Tears flowed as the service closed. That night I had a dream that I recorded the next day titled "Is This Me?"

IS THIS ME?

Are you really my body?
> How can it be
> when my leg is wooden and the knee won't bend.
> when my hand is limp and arm won't extend,
> But you say it's true,
> for better or for worse,
> I belong to you.

Are you really my mind?
> How can it be.
> When my words stay hidden inside my brain
> And memory loss makes you wonder
> If you are even mentally sane.
> But you say it's true,
> for better or worse,
> I belong to you.

Are you really my feelings?
> How can it be
> When my joy and happiness has been
> Totally usurped by grief and sadness.
> But you say it's true,
> for better or worse,
> I belong to you.

Is there anything left of me?

Anything like I use to be?

feeling in despair for all of me that is gone

forever

I cry out in agony, and then I heard---

"here I am"

I am deep within you, untouched by turmoil

    waiting to be found

I am your all enduring, ever-present spirit—

    Protected by God the Divine

Be still and listen to this God filled Spirit

    You'll find peace from turmoil and

    guidance for what to do

        for seeking life anew.

PS   From the ashes of my former self, rose the Phoenix

I was blessed by a miracle from God. I was renewed through the Holy Spirit.

I witnessed this in a dream Ash Wednesday, 1993. When I woke I had a new-found PEACE and knew that I truly found life anew. I was "healed".

That peace is still with me today, now twenty years later.

With Acceptance comes peace.

Prayer: From Philippians 4:7; and the song "Make Me a Channel"

Bless me with your peace dear God. May a sense of Gods wholeness, everything coming together for good displace all worry; and make me a channel of your peace. Amen

God is Worthy

Adoption

I was disappointed; our initial birth mother had changed her mind. I was grieving the loss of a child that I had only held in my arms briefly, and yet felt so connected to. I needed to get away and be with God. I needed quiet time desperately. I found a silent retreat camp and drove out to the site quickly. I spent the first forty eight hours acting like a child; literally throwing a temper tantrum. I kept asking God why he had allowed that to happen to me. I hadn't called the birth mother, she had called me. She had promised that I would be taking a baby home the next day. And then she had changed her mind. "Why God did you allow this to happen?"

I have heard from others who have gone on silent retreats that God still speaks, it's just that most of the time we aren't listening; too much external noise. Spouses, children, television, radios, computers, IPads and the list goes on. The world has mastered the art of keeping us so distracted that we don't hear the voice of God. It is not rocket science is it?. When we have something delicate to share with our children, spouses, significant others, do we yell over the television, radio or IPad, or do we try to find some quiet down time to have a heart to heart. I believe it is the same with a conversation with God - in the scriptures, we are told that he says "if you seek me earnestly you will find me."

Well after two days of complaining, I believe God had had enough. It was Sunday morning when I woke up early to hear Gods voice as clearly as if he was standing right next to me. He said "you want things your way and you don't get to have things your way, you get to have things my way." Oh, Ok then. That was clear enough. I packed my bags and headed home. (Part A)

God's abounding love

(Part B) The next year was a milestone birthday and this time as I reflected on my life, I knew that I knew that I knew that the only reason I was alive to speak about this birthday was because of the grace of God. I also knew that it was with God alone that I wanted to spend that birthday. So I packed my bags and headed off again to the silent retreat. This time it was different. This time I came to say thank you. It was a peaceful weekend, and I came back home refreshed and revived. I also came back home with an attitude of gratitude. My life has been blessed. God has been good to me!
It is amazing isn't it, what happens when one lives in an attitude of gratitude. There is a peace and calmness that comes over one that makes the day to day grind seem minimally manageable, and maximally trivial.

    The story could easily end here but it didn't. With this new attitude came a desire to live in gratitude with what we had, instead of frustration over what we didn't have. I mentioned this to my husband as I was wondering if pursuing the adoption journey was a sign of ingratitude. He suggested that we keep our application active at least until the adoption study expired.

    Then Gods awesomeness went on display yet again as he bestowed on us another gift. I remember the Sunday morning clearly, phones ringing one after another; my cell phone, my husband's cell phone, the home phone. I remember thinking;

"someone is trying to get a hold of us." It was true. Someone was trying to get a hold of us. A young birth mother was giving us a gift; the gift of a beautiful baby. To God be the glory.

Love in action - Our birth mothers story

(Part C) She was a single mother when she discovered she was again pregnant. She was counseled to terminate the pregnancy, but decided she couldn't and wouldn't do it. She said the adoption choice was a hard choice, but for her the right choice. She said she wanted the best for all her children and wanted our child to have everything that she was unable to provide.

Prayer: From Psalm 34

I will bless the Lord at all times. His praise will continually be in my mouth. My soul will make its boast in the Lord. The humble will hear of it and be glad. Glorify the Lord with me, and let us exalt his name together. I sought the Lord and he answered me. Amen.

God is Glorious

Daddy taught me

We were gathered around a prayer circle, four adults and one child – a toddler. No one was speaking, each adult deferring to the other. One was a preacher, one was the guest, one was the host, and one was the elder; each one deferring to the other for an unstated reason.

The silence went on for a little while when out of the silence came the sound of a toddler singing: ***"Take Glory Father, Take Glory Son, Take Glory Holy Ghost; You deserve it all."*** Amen.

I asked the three year old where she learned the song.
"My daddy taught me she said."
Out of the mouth of babes!

Prayer: From Psalm 8

Oh Lord my God how majestic is your name in all the earth. Who have set your glory above the heavens. Out of the mouth of babes and nursing infants, you have ordained praise. Amen

God is Father

Parenting

I realize that for many of us, our relationships with our earthly fathers may cause us to question God as father. I am learning that rather than wishing my imperfect father was the perfect father I wanted him to be; I can instead look up to God who is a perfect father. I can also look around to people like my brothers who although imperfect, have found ways to honor God through their parenting. From them and others, (including my own father) I put together a composite picture of what God as father might represent. He represents love.

Prayer: from Mathew 6:9-13

Father in heaven, hallowed be thy name

Thy Kingdom come, Thy will be done

On earth as it is in heaven

Please give us this day our daily bread

And forgive us our sins as we forgive those who sin against us

And lead us not into temptation

But deliver us from the evil one

For thine is the kingdom and the power and the glory forever

Amen.

Saying Goodbye to Dad

I have found even with profound faith that God loves me, loves all his children. I am grieving the loss of my father to the point that my stomach sometimes feels all twisted; however at this point of my faith journey, I have found a daily reliance on God more than ever before.

Life can throw you curve balls, tough ones. I have to admit this past year has been really tough, sad, yet in the sadness full of fun family times. Through it all, I know that God and his angels were watching over us all through the year, and still today.

April 17, 2014 my Dad, Mom and I went into the hospital for an endoscopic diagnostic procedure for my Dad. The procedure, an endoscopic retrograde cholangiopancreatography (ERCP) allows the pancreas, stomach and duodenum to be seen clearly and on x-ray. As a doctor of pharmacy and as a daughter I jumped right into the role of medical representative for my dad Cal, and mom Dorothy.

My parents had been married for forty nine years and had just returned from a two week Caribbean cruise. I noticed that my parents looked happy and relaxed after their two week cruise; bronzed by sun. I thought "wow dad looks a little thinner yet heathy - good for him." A couple of weeks later, we all met at my daughter's musical show at school; dad's tan was gone and he looked more yellow/orange. I remember thinking, that he looked jaundiced.

Turns out he had other symptoms including fatigue, elevated liver enzymes, and lack of appetite. The ERCP confirmed a pancreatic tumor. Additional testing confirmed the worst; dad had both pancreatic and lung cancer. The lung cancer had spread through his bones and he was given a prognosis of six months to a year to live. This was Easter 2014.

How does that sit with you? This was tough news for us all. He went through a couple rounds of Chemotherapy and with a break in October 2014, my husband, our four girls; my mom and dad all flew to Destin, Florida for a beautiful vacation. (A God miracle). This "Chemo Holiday" turned into lasting family memories for us all. Dad was able to take his last visit out to the beach and sit under the umbrella on the beautiful white soft sand with his grandkids around him. Thank you God for allowing this special time to happen. It was only four months later that dad would pass away.

We attended church one Sunday - my husband and our four daughters and the message was "Finding Joy in Cancer" - that hit home. God's greatest gifts coming to us in daily joy, little bits, and special moments together. My song of inspiration became "The Joy of the Lord is my Strength."

My Father died February 11, 2015. I thank God I was able to be with him and mom during his last six weeks of hospice care. He remained at their home where they were married for 49 years, raised their two kids and welcomed their grandchildren and extended family. It was beautiful to see mom and dad share a relationship "till death do us part."

Dad was a loyal family man, sometimes of few words but yet funny moments. He always showed up for family celebrations and holidays. For all those memories, I am forever thankful to my Heavenly Father and thankful for my dad Cal who now lives in heaven. My heart aches so much I cannot believe he is not here. I wish I could just hear his voice, give him a hug, sip coffee with him and play with the grandkids or watch him drive the speedboat as I waterski or the grandkids go tubing. I have so many memories of the loving loyal father that I had here on earth. I can only imagine just how much my Heavenly Father, our Savior loves me, loves you.

We are in the middle of summer activities right now, including soccer schedules for four kids, summer swim lessons, birthday parties, and cabin weekends. These joyful moments warm my heart - but I am also very thankful for the Lord God who sends his angels to give me the "peace that passes all understanding" as I grieve and miss my father and adjust to the new normal of life. My husband has been my right hand in this - he was also dad's best friend. It was a great sight to see dad and Scott connecting over the years.

A short time before dad died, my time with him was spent lying in his bed, rubbing his back, talking about old times, and reading scripture to him. I asked if he believed in God, and if Jesus was his Savior, and if he believed in heaven. His response was "Oh Yeah of course."

Cancer may have taken his earthly body but Christ claimed his heart. I know that dad is in heaven with our savior, and this brings me peace, I miss my dad a lot, as does my husband, and our kids; but we all believe that Grandpa Cal is in Heaven and cheering us on. Here's to the new normal, and Jesus being in it all over again.

Prayer: Personal Thanksgiving

Thank you Jesus for saving us all. Everyday Jesus I need your strength and your grace. Thank you for loving us. Amen.

God is Healer

This Illness is Not to Death

The call came while I was at work. Your mother is in a coma and is not expected to make it; we need you back in town. On the plane, my prayers were very simple; "Lord, I want to see my mother again; please let her be alive when I get to the hospital." I opened my bible, and it opened to the book of John Chapter 11 verse 4 "this illness is not to death." When I walked into the hospital room she opened her eyes.

She would be ill for a very long time; and we would have to fight to ensure that her caregivers did not hasten her death. A series of what were in my opinion poor medical decisions tested our faith and extended her stay. Finally however we landed in the care of a doctor and nurses whose care would nurture her back to health. She would leave the hospital alive, and would live for another ten years beyond that day. Praise be to God.

Prayer: From Psalm 30: 2 and Psalm 140: 1 -2

Lord I call to you for help. Please heal me.

Deliver us oh Lord from evil people. Rescue us from violent people who plan to trip us up. Amen.

God is Provider

The home search

It is late one evening, and I am lying in bed thinking of all that mother had been through; and realizing that she would need long term care. My prayer was simple, Lord I don't want mom in a nursing home. I want to take care of mother, but I also want my own life. So the way I see it, I am going to need an L shaped home. Mother will be on one end of the 'L' and I (and the family you will give me) on the other. Thanks in advance. Good night.

The home search did not begin for another year, and by then truth be told, I had forgotten all about my prayer; but God had not. The first part of the search was frustrating; we needed a handicapped accessible bathroom and one level living. This was hard to find. Finally, the realtor called one afternoon and said that a property that had been on the market for over a year was again available – it had been taken off the market and updated; most importantly, it had a handicapped accessible bathroom.

I am driving home from viewing the property, relatively unimpressed when I hear that still small voice inside me. 'Isn't that what you said you wanted?' And it all comes back to me; the "L" shaped home for mother and me. That was it. It had everything we needed; but before we get too far ahead of ourselves let's see what mother thinks.

I drive mother up to the house and pull up outside. "This is good" she says. "Don't you want to look inside mother I said?" "No this is it" she says.

…"Ask the father anything you want in my name – and it shall be given to you" – Jesus Christ.

Even when you forget you asked! God does not forget.
God takes care of his servants. Mom was a faithful servant of God. He would make sure her needs were met.

As a prologue; me caring for mom – that was a misnomer. When all is said and done, it was mom caring for me. The prayers, the words of wisdom, the patience, the love I received from her far exceeded the tasks that I was performing to meet her daily needs.

Prayer: From Psalm 23

The Lord is my shepherd, I shall not want

He makes me to lie down in green pastures

He leads me beside the still waters

He restores my soul

He anoints my head with oil

My cup overflows

Surely goodness and mercy shall follow me all the days of my life

And I shall dwell in the house of the Lord forever. Amen

God is Restorer

Restored back to life

A young girl's heart is very delicate because many young girls develop their self-esteem from outside influences. Peer pressure and the need to satisfy others causes many young girls to be misled into believing that sex is what makes them "a real woman" and accepted into society. I believe that this is one of the reasons young women find themselves in prostitution. This is my story.

I was just a young girl when I moved to the city for my high school education. I was young, and naïve. I had been raised in the countryside where technology was minimal. In the city, I was introduced to a lifestyle that turned my life around.

I was in eleventh grade and a virgin until my female friends brought me a movie to watch. I soon realized that this movie was more than a movie. It made my body react in a way that I had never felt before. It was a pornographic movie that showed men and women having sex.

After I watched that movie something inside started to crave for more and without knowing it, I was addicted. Instead of doing my homework after school, I would sit and watch pornographic movies. After a while, my girlfriends introduced me to some young men. Sex became normal and we would have sex in the same room with my girlfriends who had their own boyfriends. In my young mind I felt I was now a mature woman and this made me accepted in society. I was wrong.

I continued with this life style until I found out that I was pregnant. This hit me hard because I was raised in a christian home. To have a child out of wedlock was unacceptable; more so because the guy who got me pregnant was of another faith. I told my friends about my condition only to be disappointed. They forsook me and I was now in this thing all by myself. I felt so alone and even contemplated suicide.

    I finally decided that I would opt for an abortion and found my way to a facility where I had the procedure. As I was going through the surgery, I lost consciousness. I heard someone saying "we are losing her" and suddenly there was a blackout. I thought I had died. By God's mercy, after several hours a miracle happened and I was back to life. They informed me that they had removed the fetus, and that I was lucky to be alive.

    I went home but the healing took a long time. A scar was left on the inside. By God's grace however, I overcame and now I can encourage others. I can tell young women not to allow anyone to destroy your life. Run from those who want to initiate you into bad behaviors. I may have survived but you don't know if you will as I did. I believe I survived to tell you the story. You are beautiful the way you are and you don't have to destroy your precious body just to please others.

Prayer: From Psalm 139

Oh Lord you have searched me and you know me

You created my inmost being

I praise you because I am fearfully and wonderfully made.

Search me Oh God and know my heart. Test me and know my anxious thoughts. See whether I have done anything wrong, and then guide me on the road to eternal life. Amen

God is Creator

Encounters

The universe is such a wonderful place and its wonders will not cease. The bible says that the universe was created by the word of God and everything within it. When you look at it this way, God knows how and why he created us and although he created us in his own image, he made each one of us unique. John 15:5 says that "he is the vine and we are the branches." I believe that God chooses and calls us from the initial stages of our lives; however few of us notice and follow the call.

My encounters with Christ began at an early age. I was about the age of twelve, walking with my mother, on the way to attend a faith based convention. We were both praying that we would have an encounter with Christ. As we were walking, God opened my eyes and I saw the heavens open and Christ descending on clouds. I froze. It seemed that I was the only one standing there because I neither felt, nor heard, nor noticed anyone except what was before me. I knew it was Christ.

I suddenly realized that my mother was shaking me asking what was wrong. I told her what I had seen. She had not seen the same thing.

When we arrived at the convention, we heard the preacher say "those who had eyes tonight would have seen that the heavens opened." I heard my mother scream at the top of her lungs "my daughter saw the Lord tonight" and I was ushered to the front of the church for prayer.

What I learned from this encounter is that when you seek the Lord; he shows up. That is not to say that I don't face hard times. I do, and I struggle with it sometimes but when I take my eyes off the problems and concentrate on Jesus, he shows up in many ways.

Another way in which God shows up in my life is through encounters with others; for example through people who come into my life, but are only there for a moment and then are gone. I have come to believe that those people are angels who have to move on to another assignment in somebody else's life.

Some encounters occur through friends who show up and stay with my interest at heart and other encounters occur through friends who have come into my life to distract me and take me off course. I believe that the friends and moments that come into our lives to distract us can be used by God to see if we have learned to fly and soar.

Prayer from Ephesians 6:11-18

May the almighty God keep us all and open our eyes to his endless ways. Amen.

God is Near

Needing wisdom

As a young graduate I moved from Minnesota to New York to look for a job and start my career. I was staying with a friend of the family for a few weeks until I could find my own place. My friend who was a single mom with a teenage son was living in a small one bedroom apartment. The place was too small for the three of us and even though she was a very gracious hostess, living in such a small place had made it very difficult for me to concentrate on job and apartment hunting. So my priority became to search for an apartment and my goal was to find another place to live within one week.

My friend was not familiar with the city as she was a newcomer to the city herself. So I was pretty much on my own in this search. I would leave the house early in the morning, buy my coffee at the local coffee shop, check the papers, make phone calls, travel from east to west, north to south, get lost many times and come home late in the evening.

I was approaching my deadline and the following day was the last day for me to fulfill my promise to myself and find a place to move out. That evening as I was driving to see an apartment, I was so desperate that I thought to myself no matter how bad the apartment is, I will take it.

After I parked my car and walked toward the apartment, something didn't feel right. I felt scared and unsafe but I couldn't put my finger on it. The apartment to my surprise was very decent but I had this uneasy feeling about the area. The landlord told me I could move in right away as the place was vacant. His offer was very tempting but there was a voice inside me that prevented me from going forward with his offer.

I asked him to give me a few minutes; went to my car and started to pray. I asked God to give me wisdom to make the right decision. After a few minutes, I opened my glove compartment to get a tissue and saw a small dictionary that I always kept in my car. I took the dictionary in my hands, closed my eyes and started to pray "God please give me signs if I should take this apartment or walk away".

Holding that problem in my mind, I decided to open the dictionary and the third word from the bottom on the left page would be my answer. After so many years I don't remember the exact word but I do remember the definition. It said "the place where criminals hang out."

What made me decide to go to my car, to reach out for the dictionary, to select which word would be my answer and to receive such a clear answer? Call it luck, intuition or faith. All I can say is that every time I have opened my heart to communicate with God he has answered. It never fails.

So I left, and the following day the first apartment I saw became my home for a couple of years. I moved in with another young professional female who has become a very good friend of mine. That same day which was my deadline I moved out. As I was taking out some of my belongings, the postman delivered a letter which congratulated me for the new job that I was expected to start as of the following Monday. Not having a clue about the geography of New York, nervously I showed the letter to my new roommate who smiled and said how lucky I was. My commute to work would be only twenty minutes.

Later on I learned that the area in which the other apartment was located was a high crime neighborhood and had I gone against my consultation with God and moved in to that apartment my commute to work would have been close to an hour and a half!

Prayer: From Psalm 139 and 2 Kings 6:17

I thank you God that even before I say a word, you know what I need, and you are ready to answer. I pray now as Elisha prayed, please open my eyes Lord so that I may see that you are near. Amen.

God is Omnipotent (Almighty)

Emma

Everything about Emma's life is a miracle. It started at conception. Prior to conceiving Emma, I had my first pregnancy a year earlier. I had been playing tennis, experienced some blood discharge, and went to see my gynecologist. An ultra sound showed two embryos. I was carrying twins. We were so excited. My husband's side of the family has a history of twins.

Unfortunately, five weeks later I had some more complications and lost our little ones. It was one of the hardest years of my life. I wanted to know why and there were no definitive answers. I also experienced some health issues from it so when we got pregnant again, it was a surprise and obviously God's plan not mine. What I learned from the day I lost my twins and continue to learn each and every day is that God is in control not me. No matter how much I try I will never be able to know and do everything I want. It is a lesson we as parents know all too well; but that was the beginning of the journey for me.

The next part of my journey began on December 22, of that year. We had just come home from celebrating a surprise birthday party I had organized for my husband. We met a few of his closest friends for dinner and had come back to get a good night's rest before getting on a plane to fly to Arizona to be with his family for Christmas. I couldn't sleep and started to have some abdominal pain. I thought this was happening because of all the excitement and planning I had been doing. I was twenty six weeks pregnant and hadn't really had any pain in that area before. Unfortunately the contractions didn't stop and they started to get stronger. We called the obstetrician on call and they told us to go to the hospital to get this checked out. I was really nervous and upset and so was my husband. This was our second pregnancy. The other pregnancy had ended in a miscarriage and now this!

When we got there, I was immediately hooked up to a machine that monitored the number of contractions I was having and how far apart they were. It did not look good; this baby was not slowing down. So they injected me with a mild to moderate contraction drug and monitored me every thirty minutes to see how the drug was doing. Well unfortunately it didn't work so they put me on a low to moderate dose of a stronger drug. This one had a lot of side effects and you could not just go off it cold turkey you had to go down little by little. Needless to say it was quite the roller coaster ride.

Later that night or early that next morning I was told that they could not increase the potency of the drug anymore I was at my limit; if the contractions didn't stop they had no choice but to let the baby come. I started to cry. I felt so helpless. They started talking about the risks of having a baby this early and how it may or may not survive. They wanted to have me watch a video about babies that are born too early and what that would entail. I was so overwhelmed, exhausted, and upset. The only thing that kept me going was my faith in God. I prayed like I never prayed before and lifted up this little baby to Him, asking that whatever happens that he would take care of this precious gift for us.

I drifted off to sleep out of pure exhaustion and woke up with an amazing peace. I had a dream that I was at the post office mailing a letter and had a baby carrier with me and I was trying to see desperately who was in it and all I saw was a pink baby blanket with a girl inside and at that moment God spoke to me and said: "Tammy, Do not worry everything is going to be alright." (At the time we did not know it was a girl because we elected to wait and be surprised). We actually thought it was a boy because my husband comes from a family of seven boys and there is no immediate cousin that is a girl on his side. After that amazing experience I knew no matter what happened my little girl was going to be alright.

I remained in the hospital for a full two weeks as I went up and down on drugs. It was a very difficult time as we were in the hospital over Christmas and New Year's; not the best place to be for many reasons except Emma. The result was we kept that little girl in and even though I was on full bed rest I got to go home with a medication pump and have people wait on me hand and foot. It was a very humbling experience and I am very grateful to family, friends and my small group at church for their generosity and support during that difficult time. The outcome was that we were able to put off Emma's entry into this world until the thirty eighth week.

She is our miracle and continues to be a blessing and bright spot in our lives. She also continues to remind me at the sweet age of twelve that I am not in control. God is in control, and I need to look to him in every moment of everyday and rely on his power and guidance as I strive to be the best mom, wife, and woman God has made me to be.

Prayer: from the song - Now Thank We All Our God

Now thank we all our God, with hearts and hands and voices, who wondrous things hath done, in whom this world rejoices who from our mothers arms hath blessed us on our way, with countless gifts of love, and still is ours today. Amen

God is Everlasting

Life is a Marathon

I had a set of life goals that I wanted to accomplish before my fiftieth birthday. Running a marathon was a goal I had set when I was thirty five and fifty was a long ways away. However, here I was on my forty eighth birthday with fifty just right around the corner, and I had not yet run a marathon.

Turns out my church was gathering a group together to run a half marathon to raise money for clean water in a 'sister' community. I decided this was my chance; and a half marathon would have to suffice. I had always wondered why the new testament writers described the christian race as running a marathon. What were the parallels? I wanted to find out. Here is what I learned.

Lesson 1: In life, run your own race

At the beginning of the race there was a lot of excitement as everyone took off running. Initially I thought to take off with the rest of the pack, but then reminded myself that I had not once run a seven minute mile during training, and the beginning of a thirteen mile run was not the time to find out if I was up to the task. I slowed down and paced myself to run as I had trained.

By the end of the first mile, I was bringing up the rear of the pack. I again considered changing my strategy but instead settled in to do what I had trained for and run my own race. It was the right thing to do, by the time I got to the two mile mark, there were people on the side of the road throwing up, and an ambulance carrying someone away. They had petered out two miles into the race.

Life is a marathon *– **Run your own race** –* Do not covet your neighbor's house, car…… or running prowess.

Lesson 2: Rest when you need to

My neighbor, who is twenty years older than I am, became an accomplished marathon runner after he retired. He gave me some advice that he learned from his first race. He said, don't forget to rest.

I am getting tired and decided to ***stop and rest*** and stretch. Feels crazy in the middle of a marathon, but that is what I needed to do. So I did, and it was enough to keep me going, sustain me for another while and keep me from cramping up.

Lesson 3: There are helpers along the way

Seven miles into the race I am feeling very good but by the eighth mile I am not feeling good at all. I am tired and find myself slowing down into a walk. This is followed by a rush of negative thoughts. "How did I get myself into this?" "Why am I doing this?" "Five more miles to go" "This is so boring – aagh."

Just in time, along comes the three hour pacer. "You are not going to let me get ahead of you, are you?" he says. I guess not. My goal was to be done in three hours. He ran with me; forced me to keep pace until I was buoyed up again and then he dropped back to help someone else who was growing weary from the journey.

Support comes from the most unexpected places. Accept it!

Lesson 4: Angels are cheering you on – you may not see them but they are ever present.

I have come up past the eleventh mile. I look up and I can see the end of the race is to my right. Unfortunately the race route directs me away from the finish line to the left. I am frustrated, and so very tired. I have to keep my eyes down because if I look up I will quit. I hear the cheers of bystanders encouraging me on….and it helps. I don't look up even though some of them call me by name. I assume they are reading my name from my race badge. They tell me I am doing a good job. They tell me I am almost there. I believe them. I have to. I can't stop because if I do, I will quit. I can't quit; so close to the end. I am so grateful for those 'angels'; most, if not all of them complete strangers to me. Their words of encouragement cheer me on; one step at a time.

Lesson 5: It is always darkest before the dawn

I am in tears, completely spent; I finally look up to ask the lady who just cheered me on how much further I would have to go. She must have seen my pain because she seemed moved. She tells me to hang in there and just get past the corner. "Just to the corner she says. As soon as you turn the corner, you will see the finish line." Just to the corner I keep telling myself; almost in tears. Just to the corner. I am in such pain – just to the corner. Well she was right. I turned the corner and there it was; the finish line and scores of people, that I didn't know, still waiting to cheer me home. I am buoyed and cross the finish line. "Congratulations" I hear. "Well done." I don't know who is speaking but there are smiling faces wishing me well as I cross the finish line. I check my time. I finished my race just in time 2 hours 59 minutes and 57 seconds.

One day, another day; I don't know when, I will finish another race. Just in time. And once again, I pray that there will be scores of angels waiting to cheer me home; and my savior waiting with a smile saying "well done."

Prayer: From the song - Lead on Oh King Eternal

Lead on Oh King Eternal till sins fierce wars shall cease and lowliness shall whisper the sweet amen of peace. Thy cross is lifted o'er us, we journey in its light; the crown awaits the conquest lead on Oh God of might. Amen.

God is Awesome

Miracle Child

I always wanted 6 kids, like my mother had. I had my first child at the age of twenty nine, well and healthy. Two years after, decided to try for more and proceeded to have a pregnancy every year after that for the next five years. Each pregnancy ended in an ectopic or miscarriage. Each one was devastating. I finally decided things needed to be checked out to see what the problem was.

My fears came to fruition, after tests were done, I was told both my tubes were completely 100% blocked; not even regular fluid was getting through, so the chances of ever having another child the regular way were nil. I remember leaving the hospital and just sitting in my car totally devastated and wondering and asking God why? No answers were forth coming then, so I pulled myself together and went back to work in a total daze.

This continued for the next few months. I continued to pray and the words that kept coming to me were from a song: "Let it go, lay it down, leave it at the feet of Jesus." Eventually I did and was at peace with it.

Five years later, at the ripe young age of 42, I figured out I was pregnant. I thought it was early menopause; it did not even occur to me that I was pregnant. I was five weeks along, and the ectopic pregnancies and pregnancies and miscarriages usually happened between six and eight weeks, so I nervously kept it to myself for the next three weeks and prayed about it. I thanked God after the eight weeks but did not go in for a checkup till I was more than three months along; as in the past when I had gone in earlier, I had lost the baby. I know totally paranoid.

Lo and behold four days after my check up, excruciating abdominal pains started (signs of a miscarriage or ectopic pregnancy) and continued for the next three days straight; paranoia…I think not. Talked to my sister, she said it could be Braxton Hicks contractions which were normal, but not usually so early. I calmed down a bit but I stayed horizontal and prayed like never before that weekend.

The pain finally subsided and the next two months went relatively smoothly. We had now told everyone. At this stage, I was called in to the hospital and was put in a room and briefed with every single horrific thing that could happen or possibly go wrong with this pregnancy, since I was over thirty five. They wanted to put a needle in me to check the amniotic fluid to see if the child could have Down syndrome or any other number of things. I politely told them none of the tests would be happening; that if the Lord was able to help me get pregnant when science said it was impossible, then 1) I was going to trust God, 2) that whatever came out of me I would gladly, gratefully and joyfully accept and 3) I wasn't going to allow anyone to poke and prod me to wreck anything. This was my miracle baby, and no one was going to mess it up.

At seven months, I went in again as I was bleeding. Ultrasounds and more tests were done. All was well, but they determined that there was a slight rupture in the placenta wall, so I had to take it easy so it would not get any worse and cause further issues. I took all of this to the Lord in prayer.

Finally came to term, and had my scheduled C-section (not my choice), but my miracle perfect daughter was born, just a bit early. Ten perfect fingers, a full head of hair, and perfect lung capacity. I thanked God over and over again for this wonderful miracle. Because it was in his own time and when he knew I would need this the most. She is my constant companion and I thank God every day for these wonderful children he has seen fit to bless me with, I pray that I raise them according to his will, for his kingdom.

Prayer from Psalm 18

I love you, LORD, my strength. The LORD is my rock, my fortress and my deliverer; my God is my rock, in whom I take refuge. I called to the LORD, who is worthy of praise. In my distress I called to the LORD. I cried to my God for help. From his temple he heard my voice. My cry came before him, into his ears. He reached down from on high and took hold of me. He drew me out of deep waters. The LORD lives. Praise be to my Rock. Exalted be God my Savior. Amen

God is Faithful

A Cure for Busy-ness

It's always hard to say when a story began, but I know part of my story began the day I met Paul, our mission's pastor. At the new member's class, he explained he was from the Congo, and grew up there and in the States. I introduced myself and told him I had trained with a retired missionary doctor in the Congo. He was a big mentor to me and I had been scheduled to go to Congo with him but the trip got cancelled because of the upheaval there in the late 1990s. Then I remembered right then and there he had been with the Presbyterian Church. Paul asked me who it was, I told him, and he exclaimed, "Uncle Walt! I grew up with his daughters in the Congo." I felt like God was tapping me on the shoulder.

I told Paul that I wanted to go to Congo. He looked at me with my three young kids like I was crazy. "I speak French" I told him. I was hoping this would give me some bonus points in his eyes. He later told me he thought to himself, how is this going to work?

Fast forward one year; my husband and I were having some issues, and briefly separated. I went to a very wise counselor who worked with me on forging ahead with reconciliation. One issue we had was that I was not always acknowledging or making my needs known in our marriage. We discussed "rules for reconciliation." It seemed to me out of the blue at the time, but she asked me one thing that I had always wanted to do but had not been able to. I blurted out, "Going to Africa" before I could even think about it.

I really wanted reconciliation, but I also knew it was important to have my needs met in our marriage, not just my husbands or the kids. When I told my husband, he looked at me like I was crazy but agreed. I think he thought I would forget; but I started going to Congo meetings and finding out more information and planning how my sister and in laws could help him take care of the children.

Everything fell into place from there. Tap again from God, probably the biggest one. Another physician, who turned out to be the other obstetrician/gynecologist who went on my trip, was at the "Go team" booth for Congo. She was so encouraging, and didn't think I was silly for considering a trip when I had young children. Another tap from God.

Things were kind of on autopilot, but one thing I hadn't addressed prior to committing 100% to the trip was figuring out my work schedule. I had told a few of my colleagues that I was considering a trip, but had not yet officially requested hospital call coverage from them.

I was at a meeting early that summer--the trip was planned for the Fall--and one of my partners walked up to me and said, "I heard you are thinking about a mission trip. Do you need anyone to take any call?" I said, "Yes, the Tuesday before Thanksgiving." He said, "Done." I said, "Don't you need to ask your wife or look at your calendar?" He said, "I'll make it work". That has never, ever happened to me before, and I doubt it ever will again. I thought to myself--I guess I'm going to Africa! Tap.

I did have some doubts along the way. I had been warned about spiritual warfare, and part of me felt crazy for going someplace that is potentially so unsafe. I had a dream in the spring that I was in the Congo and that I died. This was very scary to me, because I was already uneasy about separating from my children. I spoke with another very wise woman, my older sister, who pointed out to me that God would not be sending me such an evil dream. I realized she was right and that immediately gave me courage. Tap.

Our senior pastor gave a sermon somewhere in there about one way you demonstrate your faith is by doing something the rest of the world thinks is crazy. That was so true for me. Before and after my trip, I can't believe how many people literally came up to me and said, "Why are you doing this?" It led to opportunity for great testimony; I wish I had used it more.

I learned two main things with my experience: One: with God, anything is possible, even if you think it is impossible. Two: (this was so unexpected for me) I learned about the importance of the Sabbath. The importance of taking time for my spiritual growth; taking time for just me. I could not believe that thousands of miles from home, where I had gone to serve; God gave me my first true hours--long quiet time that I could remember. How utterly cool! At the time I needed a supportive family, a family that would help care for my children. I needed two weeks' vacation and someone who could cover my duties while I was gone. I needed the assurance from God that this was truly His plan for me. This all fell into place for me which was incredible.

One thing that I learned in the Congo is that I get so self-absorbed in my busy-ness, that I don't take time to recognize ways I can be supportive to others around me. So my prayer is simply, for God's guidance and support in recognizing this and to help me intercede, and to help cure me of my busy-ness; just as he taught me in the Congo.

Prayer: From Hebrews 4

Lord, I thank you that your goal for me is that I rest in you. Help me to receive this promise in faith. Amen.

God is Grace

A New Life

Sharing my faith story had been a difficult one because it's not even close to what I thought my life would be like. When I was a little girl we attended a nice Church and I had wonderful parents who instilled strong morals and values. I felt church was more of a thing that you should attend to check it off on our "good family" list. I believe that if I had been told about the power of a relationship with Jesus, I might not have made all the bad choices and mistakes that added up early on in my life. One thing I do know is that my mistakes are also what ultimately lead to Jesus and his powerful hold in my life now.

After College, I was hired as a Flight Attendant. I was lucky to gain a spot on the list to be based and live in Honolulu. The summer before I left, I had a casual fling with a guy. Life was great; parties, friends, bars, dating and a new exciting job.

A few weeks after moving to Hawaii I found out I was pregnant. The news was devastating to me. My first thought was the disappointment my parents, friends and family would have (I was not in a relationship). I believed that I could not handle a baby or even the pregnancy.

I also knew that one of my friends who had an abortion seemed to be fine and had moved on. I called the guy who got me pregnant, and of course there was no hesitation in his desire for an abortion. He sent the money right away.

The same week that all of this was happening my employer had to send some of us out of town on temporary duty for ten days. I started to mentally break down. I called our emergency employee assistance line and they connected me with someone to talk to who eventually got me in touch with an abortion clinic.

October 30th, 1990 I took the life of my baby. I was 24 years old and at least 8 to 10 weeks pregnant. I took the hotel van to the abortion clinic and a taxi back, I was all by myself. The procedure was awful, it hurt more then they told me it would, so cold and fast. I remember getting a beer that night in the hotel bar and looking around at the other patrons and Halloween decorations thinking, "Nobody knows what I just did"! But I knew-and it felt like a deep ache, a hole and a void.

I didn't have a very strong faith so turning to God was not much help. I looked to other things to take away the pain. I jumped right into a relationship with a Marine, he found out right away that I had an abortion because even from our first date the norm was having sex and I had to turn him down because of issues with heavy bleeding. Our relationship, despite trying hard, was never very healthy. We stayed together for two and half years. Soon after it ended I met and married a guy who brought me back to Minnesota but the marriage only lasted about a year.

Now divorced, I was completely broken; after making such stupid decisions, I was desperate to find "true happiness". I hit bottom and opened up to my parents. I told them everything.

What was revealed to me at that time was I needed to pray and reach out to Jesus. My mom and sister had been attending Bible study at church; I noticed the impact learning God's word was having on them and I wanted a piece of it too. Within a short time I was taking a study called "The Search for Significance". It was perfect. I got a deep sense of The Lords presence. After a few months I found myself giving my heart over and began trusting in Jesus with my life.

    A gift that came out of this study was the suggestion from our leader for me to attend a local post-abortion support group. I went head strong into the first week of the group determined to make sure that I would not cave to the fact that I had taken a life! I was still running away from the truth about the abortion. I wanted to believe that I hadn't done anything that bad.

    The group, called Conquerors revealed to me God's grace and by the end of twelve weeks I was ready to receive and believe God's forgiveness. At the closing of our session a funeral was planned for our babies and we were given the chance to read a letter to our child. As I finished my letter I could feel the physical weight being lifted off my shoulders, like a rush of something leaving my body. God was releasing that burden.

    I married my wonderful husband in 1997. We struggled with infertility for several years, enduring an ectopic pregnancy and miscarriage. I had to deal with feelings that God was punishing me that would creep in because of my brokenness. But Jesus kept showing me his grace.

    Right after the events of September 11 we found out we were pregnant with our daughter. When she was nine months old we were surprised by another pregnancy. But when I was twenty nine weeks along with our son, I was rushed to the hospital with pre-term labor and may have delivered that night. The date was October 30th 2003-exactly 13 years after I'd had my abortion. They stabilized the situation and The Lord used the next six weeks in the hospital to reveal that now I was having a chance at saving the life inside me this time and to lean on him. God has a way of working for his glory!

In my abortion story experience it seems to never end but I see the fruits it is actually producing and one of those fruits was to meet up with the man who fathered the baby, now twenty five years ago. I had to trust God's plan in our meeting and go with no expectations. I had always thought he had moved on without any feelings or regret. But to my pleasant surprise his life had been affected and he was sad for the loss of life and the impact it had on some of his relationships and feelings. I was able to walk away with a sense of peace and understanding. I continue to pray for him and his healing because it took both of us to end up in the situation to begin with.

I will end with another fruit. It is the opportunity to now tell and share my story without hesitation, embarrassment and self-hatred because I'm forgiven by Jesus, who always loved me, even when I didn't know him. This does not mean that I don't have grief when it comes to past decisions but I believe I have Jesus in my life totally because of them.

I am now able to tell people that despite once taking a life, I now have a new life with Jesus in my heart.

Prayer: From Titus 3

Lord, I receive the new life that our savior Jesus poured out so generously. I praise you Jesus for restoring my relationship to God. Amen.

Do you have a story of God's love demonstrated in your life that you want to share? Email us at **Godislovestories@gmail.com**

Bibliography:

All scripture verses were taken from the New International Version, The New King James, and the Message version as retrieved from www.biblegateway.com

Songs mentioned in this book include:

Have faith in God when your pathway is lonely
Words by Baylus Benjamin McKinney
Lyrics retrieved from:
http://www.hymnary.org/text/have_faith_in_god_when_your_pathway_is_1

I need thee every hour
Words by Annie Hawks
Lyrics retrieved from:
ttp://www.hymnsite.com/lyrics/umh397.sht

Lead on Oh King Eternal
Words by Ernest Shurtleff
Lyrics retrieved from:
http://www.cyberhymnal.org/htm/l/e/leadonok.htm

Make me a Channel of your peace
Words attributed to St. Francis of Assisi
Lyrics retrieved from: http://www.breadsite.org/lyrics/407.htm

Now Thank we all our God

Words by: Martin Rinkar;

Translated to English by Catherine Winkworth

Lyrics retrieved from:

http://www.cyberhymnal.org/htm/n/o/nowthank.htm

Banner Over Me is Love

Words from: The book of Solomon

Lyrics retrieved from: http://www.childrenssonglyrics.com/c/100-childrens-christian-songs-lyrics/577-his-banner-over-me-is-love.html

Have Faith in God

Have faith in God when your pathway is lonely;
He sees and knows all the way you have trod.
Never alone are the least of His children;
Have faith in God, have faith in God.

Have faith in God when your prayers are unanswered;
Your earnest plea He will never forget.
Wait on the Lord trust His Word and be patient;
Have faith in God, He'll answer yet.

Have faith in God in your pain and your sorrow;
His heart is touched with your grief and despair.
Cast all your cares and your burdens upon Him;
and leave them there, oh, leave them there

Have faith in God though all else fail about you;
Have faith in God, He provides for His own.
He cannot fail though all kingdoms shall perish;
He rules, He reigns, upon His throne

Chorus:
Have faith in God, He's on His throne;
Have faith in God, He watches o'er His own.
He cannot fail, He must prevail;
Have faith in God, have faith in God.

I need thee every hour

I need thee every hour, most gracious Lord;
no tender voice like thine can peace afford.

I need thee every hour; stay thou nearby;
temptations lose their power when thou art nigh.

I need thee every hour, in joy or pain;
come quickly and abide, or life is vain.

I need thee every hour; teach me thy will;
and thy rich promises in me fulfill.

I need thee every hour, most Holy One;
O make me thine indeed, thou blessed Son.

Chorus:
I need thee, O I need thee;
every hour I need thee;
O bless me now, my Savior, I come to thee.

Lead on, O King Eternal

Lead on, O King eternal,

The day of march has come;

Henceforth in fields of conquest

Thy tents shall be our home.

Through days of preparation

Thy grace has made us strong;

And now, O King eternal,

We lift our battle song.

Lead on, O King eternal,

Till sin's fierce war shall cease,

And holiness shall whisper

The sweet amen of peace.

For not with swords' loud clashing,

Nor roll of stirring drums;

With deeds of love and mercy

The heavenly kingdom comes.

Lead on, O King eternal,

We follow, not with fears,

For gladness breaks like morning

Where're Thy face appears.

Thy cross is lifted over us,

We journey in its light;

The crown awaits the conquest;

Lead on, O God of might.

Make me a channel of your peace.

Make me a channel of your peace.
Where there is hatred let me bring your love.
Where there is injury, your pardon, Lord
and where there's doubt, true faith in you.

Make me a channel of your peace
Where there's despair in life, let me bring hope
Where there is darkness, only light
And where there's sadness, ever joy.

Make me a channel of your peace
It is in pardoning that we are pardoned
In giving to all men that we receive
And in dying that we're born to eternal life.

Chorus:
Oh, Master grant that I may never seek
So much to be consoled as to console
To be understood as to understand
To be loved as to love with all my soul.

Now Thank We All Our God

Now thank we all our God, with heart and hands and voices,
Who wondrous things has done, in Whom this world rejoices;
Who from our mothers' arms has blessed us on our way
With countless gifts of love, and still is ours today.

O may this bounteous God through all our life be near us,
With ever joyful hearts and blessèd peace to cheer us;
And keep us in His grace, and guide us when perplexed;
And free us from all ills, in this world and the next

All praise and thanks to God the Father now be given;
The Son and Him Who reigns with Them in highest Heaven;
The one eternal God, whom earth and Heaven adore;
For thus it was, is now, and shall be evermore.

His Banner over Me is Love

The Lord is mine and I am His, His banner over me is love (x3)
He brought me to His banqueting table; His banner over me is love
He lifted me up into heavenly places; His banner over me is love
He is the vine and we are the branches; His banner over me is love
Jesus is the Rock of my salvation; His banner over me is love
There's one way to peace through the power of the cross;
His banner over me is love

Made in the USA
Middletown, DE
13 July 2015